widewide.world to unwind

Poetry in the unraveling

by

Joe Bisicchia

ISBN: 978-81-8253-765-1

First Edition: 2021
Rs. 200/-

Cyberwit.net
HIG 45 Kaushambi Kunj, Kalindipuram
Allahabad - 211011 (U.P.) India
http://www.cyberwit.net
Tel: +(91) 9415091004
E-mail: info@cyberwit.net

Printed at Repro India Limited.

Acknowledgements

for the manuscript

widewide.world to unwind

"needing refill" – published by *Fib*, Muse-Pie Press, 2016

"world goes round" – published by Chronogram Magazine, 2018

"singing to the stars" – published by Writing Knights Press, *Grand Showcase*, 2018

"fields of the rich" – published by Grand Little Things, 2020

"geography" – published by Golden Walkman Magazine, 2020

"countenance" – published by Fleas on the Dog, 2021

Contents

widewide.world

Sky confuses, too often sliced by arrows. Stakes are high.
Time is a tyrant. And we go big as a dot. But lives go far
more deep than any high definition screen, somewhere

intertwined beneath the pixels. We share a carousel, and
hold heaven at its mane. And perhaps then, we may know
very well the surface we share here as a big enough place,

a run far further than where the sun rises and falls within
a brass carousel ring, as wide instead as each soul is infinite
beyond a face, as near as the period at the end of a sentence.

Writers take their turns to pen of this expansive residence.
I humbly acquiesce, but my ink shall fall small here.
Take my hand. Steady it.

And here we are on a dot in the middle of the wide sky.
And here we are.
Yes, here we are…

no stone unturned

We shall boost our poems like an ongoing strengthening.
Let us see what we might find underneath ready to rise.

Gather and lift the stones.
Read poems with me.

We go sturdy as a home and circle ourselves with things, fallen.
See how we have a love-hate with broken things, hidden, found.

Perhaps, we look for a patch of earth ever available with space
so to live forever within a wall and be lost without a trace.

Then, we might unearth our dead man pockets to be remembered
lined with prayers that rattle like rosary beads despite all the dust.

And from time to time then we then might find time with velocity
to see what lingers ever still of neighbors and ourselves.

And, by grace, we shall still be found by some kind of mercy.
So, no use in hiding under a big fat thumb. Choose to love.

Fathom and find us under all the words.
Read poems with me.

packaging the world

Wrapped gift sits.
Here it is.
Just sits.
Unopened,
the present.

Pound by pound, a big place.
Spacious dreams in grams.
Each face.

We dye our eggs.

We wonder
our wonder
on the inside.

Together,
what might we find?

What's inside an open mind?

How might we start
by opening the heart?

needing refill

Parched
jar,
just clay.

The ladle,
just unfilled metal.

And a hollow heart, just the world.

Published by Muse-Pie Press Fib Review, 2016

world goes round

And once again, ephemeral goes our night sky, yet not.
Effervescence remains. The glow of stars.
Our hearts.

For those who may be in the dark, to help you out,
we are at your disposal to solve any doubt that may arise.
This is what we shall do:

we shall go hand in hand to horizon and pull for tomorrow.
And while we do, we'll take our time to admire the ceiling,
sharing this feeling of our place in space beyond all sorrow.

Published by Chronogram Magazine, 2018

one earth

So many suns have come and gone,
we may do ourselves a favor and simplify them

as only one.

And then welcome it, as it is,
and its faithful return.

And think of ourselves throughout all of time,
as such simplified matter, timeless as one.

Earth rolls,
and so much energy is measured in joules.

Bogs the mind as we walk our daily path,
as we meet and greet, and take a seat,

not falling off the face of the earth,
but by somehow, miraculously, getting by.

We can simplify this as it is.
Or, better yet, just be grateful for eternal life.

By grace, be open to how this came to be—

Today, so many lives shall be born.
Today, so many lives shall die.

Shall rise.

bricklayer

So much has come apart, to rebuild upon.
Smell the must of a thousand years
                    and the newness of the mortar at the trowel.
                    Feel the leather of thy hand and
bring together the then and now.
All the world's pyramids stand up, and the walls lift
                    human logic in the shelter and divide,
                    the shoulders holding up the veil,
the thresholds under the lintels,
the jambs onto the fields.
                    So much is molded in us from the dust,
                    every new day from the clay.

hallowed ground

The soul passes through geography.
They bombed a cemetery.

Only dirt.
To them, hollowed and now ready.

No more than an expanded mass grave,
a carpet to hide all our world under it.

A child's eyes had long gazed this place.
And lo,

Queen of Heaven still stands here,
just as she remembers.

geography

On the way to tomorrow,
on the way to the world,
we wait. And yet move.
Time and today take place.
Age craters our face.
Remnants circle the drain.
And we move on.
It is the way of the world
as it extraordinarily spins—
to surrender to grace.
Grace gives its ground.
It enjoys unveiling itself.
So goes Love.
See it, as here and beyond.
Unmistaken as eternal.
This is its manifest destiny,
as if therein is the very gift
right there in the face,
the presence of Love.
The whole way.

Published by Golden Walkman Magazine, 2020

manifest destiny

Land of your birth, I am me, for you.
I am earth.

There will be occasion, no doubt,
you will bulldoze me.

Yet, for most of my ground,
simply the graceful will plant with plough.

Still, in reverse, in weeds, seems to me,
you far too long linger through all the debris.

Maybe one day you can look at me
not seeing separate patch in separate dirt,
but seeing what can last.

For a superior scene, by grace,
why not make Manifest Destiny,
not of pieces of me
but of peace?

grace in greatness

She has foul fingernails. Lengthy and soiled.
I am a loser for forgetting she only has one arm.
No other hand to clip the wild, overrun landscape.
Nature is who she is, and she takes me on her way.

Yes, she takes my hand, and I feel the texture.
We follow the blueprint of our future on our skin.
Valleys move at immeasurable speed unrolling
as if motionless the present in our fullness of time.

Hand in hand, face to face, we dance her earth.
We might not notice a permanent trace in sand,
but see it surely, our stop upon the grain of granite.
She gracefully smiles, and we begin again.

territorial

We hold onto turf,
careful of eyes so deceived
like double checking inmates at night,
lest they leave.

Despite coyote's persistent howl,
often just a din, and inevitably a victim
to hidden crickets who own the night,
we hold onto turf.

So much comes to pass like scurrying leaves,
the wind, and all our rigid and intrepid selves.
So much drifts.
And slips through our hands.

Still, each facet of earth's face regenerates.
Sunrise approves yet another landscape
with a kiss.
And we are held.

Somehow each in a different way,
yet each somehow the same,
we move and have our being
as we hold tight the passing overhead.

snow globe

Yes, sometimes things get shaken up.

Even then,
as we wonder what hand we live under
to allow this, our mishmash of life, we get by.
Even then,
something about us does seem so very right.

Life has a way of a lift and a good mix,
evidenced most especially in our swirl,
here in our shared encircled world
midst our countless visual gifts,
and the sky's mesmerizing fingerprints.

limit

We bend and shape paper planes
but have not yet have flown our own way
to heaven,
if heaven indeed is a flyable place.

Here, we have our gravity.
It is a world that loses itself to us,
its curve, crossbeam, speck.
Its lines to permanence drift from our heads,
yet stays the meaning more than what is said,
as if only the world instead.

And we make our way here upon this place
into boundless space unleashed by grace
by giving our tomes to more than parchment.

sign of the crossing

A billboard to the right says goodbye
after its short-lived hello
as the green beacon ahead abruptly goes yellow. Then red.

After such a lifetime of a long, long drive, we finally break
into pieces as our station wagon screeches to stay inbounds
and does, despite the tossed bobbleheads.

We have arrived to slippery end of sky where we will all fall
over the side of the earth.

Maybe now is finally time to believe in flight.

well-traveled

Maybe curiosity and presentation can bend conversation
if along with willingness,
if not eagerness to discover, if a spacious soul has space for it,
all the depth that may enlighten the valley
simply in learning our similarity with others.

Heretofore unknown family is near as sisters and brothers
here and there
where we all might now go forth no longer to fear darkness
as we count our sheep,
as we peacefully sleep, tossing our separated miles and miles.

countenance

Going to the night, all this space awaits. This space,
this face at mine. At its edge, the cyclone fence is like teeth.
Sign is posted and posed, its lettering with a frown nonetheless
but maybe a surface only afraid,

maybe mean, maybe a sphinx wishing to level in an instant
a guillotine rather than simply a warming hello or a
long linear defense. It rattles. She smiles a facade in breeze
and speaks of things. If only I could read

her language, but I can dream, and allow myself to believe
in my dreams. Maybe we live in the bleakest night of hell,
but there are holes to be seen under so many stars, signs
of peace, a sweeping smile on a familiar face.

Such a grace might be the most powerful thing in the world.
Somehow seems we overlook the icons of our day,
the lone happy face, and then stare at the long teeth
of a roaring lion, but only when it is fast asleep.

Published by *Fleas on the Dog*, 2021

death valley

There is similar history to Mother Nature's face.
Frays to the weight.

Even in the coolness of night.

Despite the hidden bowling ball in her leather bag,
she grimaces that loving smile, her way of might.

landmark

Humankind has a familiar face. More than any characters

in a name, there is character. I am. And we all are. Muses
on our journey.

And a name aflame, we are, and an image repeated, repeated,
repeated on the way.

This is us hand in hand at a mile post. Somehow that is enough
in knowing where

we are.

mountains cry

Time cuts through them,
all the faces that have settled into places.
Seeing what springs from even a poem,
and what flows down Petit Dru and hills, is us.
And we all have looked for the Fountain of Youth.

And have worn maps of Italy as boots, foreign
from everywhere swinging our pick hammers at heat.
Immigrants time and time again meet the Muscogee.
And there was that day her native face opened her spirit.
I saw it.

Old and precious, she had eagerly lived her range.
Now she was as a child, in the wet eyes and smile.
Her upper teeth like a new picket fence.
No lower teeth, just a mound over a waiting trench.
She threw a rock up at Sisyphus, a message to send.

Said she only wished to remind her friend to love.
So much grows old and dies, but what remains?
From then on to now, placing a new old face,
we never go surprised at what springs
from stone.

erosion

I am here. Yet,
so much breaks away, the rocket boosters of my past.
My heart from my chest. The soul soars with spirit.
I may now see the horizon not afar but all along here
at my feet. I bend down and grasp grains of sand and

feel the essence of what lasts. So much was, and is
innermost unbreakable, despite air swooped overhead.
I leap across oceans, to the light, and there is no fear,
no wearing away of the soul when walking grounded,
here to heaven.

trajectory

Goes the carousel unceasingly, constant
ever still steady,
the indestructible smile
unmistakable in the blur,
as too somehow
the teardrop wearing the cheek, all we are
as human.

world upon our backs

The lamp shade has aged transparent,
while the chair just sits there in the dark,
for the artificial light only lives so long.

There is a burnt motorcycle on our sidewalk.
A skeleton now standing like a dog mannequin.
Was speed, now rusted bones in the breeze.

Evel Knievel and I tangle our tails
as well as our hopeful dreams for this world.
Perhaps we will unite at last, or collapse.

Perhaps wither of thirst with empty tanks.
Perhaps die with dirt upon our leathered skin
and remain as the dirt; we are like two cliffs.

Perhaps, we can forge our path in this world,
and move out of each other's way a chasm,
and maybe even levitate over all the space.

Perhaps, instead, though a turtle, gravitate,
become unified with others and levitate
as this place moves its pace and we give in.

Perhaps at the horizon all of heaven awaits
each one by one, by all as one, an embrace
here upon this bridged place we can span.

All of this is heavy.
The grace part makes it ever so light.
Like a feather we all are, if we know we can.

busy sky

not all dreams land
some fly and fly and
savor the ride to somewhere
to where there is no land
and become as they are
more precious than a star
a feather and feather and

feather along the way
trust is the way of the bridge
over the precipice
at the foot, in the wing
lost myself somewhere
inside of me
only to find myself

somewhere
somewhere in the helping
of another precious being
carrying a dream
upon my fallen feathers
now aloft in the sky
on the way to somewhere

roll away the world

What if heaven could be near as now? Our face and face are here in our lowly doldrums where ox and ass are feeding. Maybe heaven is a far off place, far as our unfastened hearts in the disarray of our own hay right here in broad daylight. You smile and so soon I notice the sunset's light just across Bethlehem Pike just as it was the same way for the Minsi Indians before it was Pennsylvania Route 309 Philly to Bethlehem. You take my hand yet again as we walk to Easter dinner at Andy's Diner, sit at our booth, and with price already paid, we later leave an empty tomb, ever full.

singing to the stars

I find it in my voice box deep in the dark of my cellar,
at first only a whisper.
It asks for the vast outdoor sky above our small world.
    And so,

we go for a walk and talk.
And, at the park, fly a kite, despite it soon being night.

Next to the constellations, it tells me
while sometimes it needs to stretch its legs
it feels good to intermingle in the twinkle of the lights.

I often long for this pause, this starry respite
when I can hear what my voice is looking for.

I hold on tight to the string.

Published by Writing Knights Press, *Grand Showcase*, 2018

high tension

taut, we are taut our wires way up high

are pulled, pulled tight. we reach, we reach.

connect, bind, times overwhelmed. we hold

the world, all this yarn, all the voices spun

one by one by one by everyone needing

unraveling. needing to be taut remembering

where we start, and to where we go.

tightly wound

Wires strung across the wide land.
Over the hills.
Under the seas.
Down the narrow streets.
Lugging and tugging.

Goes our hope, ever happening.
Goes our ever wide belief.
Goes our need for each other.
Goes the landscape parchment,
love letters holding us together.

All that acreage, the bandage
over our wounded hearts unravels
frontier of our horizon.
We let go as the milky sky unwinds
today into tonight into tomorrow.

We let go to fate,
but we hold onto each other.
And the thread makes its way
weaved with great ease
like leaves to trees in spring.

aisle runner

It portrays the way, but can trip up a passerby. Only so wide, it can only do so much. It is just a long fabric, rolled out. Here comes the bride. She runs, or hides, or unrolls her life before her, step by step. The world makes its way. And all eyes see the prize. She looks forward, and down, and upward, and maybe all around. Sees the world is more than fabric. It is textured by more than what must be afterward rolled away. Love is underneath with steady feet. What does not matter is pulled away in an instant while all the glasses and dishes stay in place. Love of life allows this, as the world itself rolls away, and lovers look into each other's eyes, and commit.

yarn

we are only upon the world
not of the world
where our fishbowl orbs open wide
to the glass image of ourselves
and to the patterned wallpaper of others
until we unravel deeper and finally see souls
and see ourselves within the pattern
and see the heaven from which we belong
and see God with us all along

kitchen window

This ball of spool of ours is compact and skintight.
Backyard yarn not yet easily unraveled, our world.
There is this suddenly noticed orange upon the sill,
and the table knife awaits to learn if land is flat.

Soon, the found smiles framed by grinds, ours
by time, by time is spread all over this here world.
And there, here, we are all children amidst a spray
of morning. Here we are indeed, in our here world.

We are not just the future, but the present, not lost,
but found. All around. Shared, no longer unopened.
In many ways proof itself the world is indeed round.
If not, the daily fruit would stay on sill motionless.

magic carpet

For ease of use,
the world wraps and unwraps, evolves and revolves around me.
Look at my hands and how they have served me,
and see.

Look at the marvels of me,
the work of individual grain, and see the power of individual
humanity.

I can carry the world.

But I also can use a hand to help me carry this rug up from the
cellar.

soon to cinder

In our small town of Watertown, we run the many paths.
And so much moves. And yet, soon stays like mud. Past
seems so much like a life long gone. I think sometimes
we find ourselves back at the slowly melting tombstones,
touching and eroding the etching. And we might wave away
a hand regarding our creek, the bridge, as our run is often
not as fun as simply wetting our feet as the water walks.

But now again so soon all pastes dry to eventual dust. And
yet, even though we forget, and even though dull, numb,
still maybe the ghosts know that our minds drift away
with the soot in the breeze. And maybe the heavy sky bends
around a distant water tower, our found power. It draws
quicker, the past, and upon this we shall run after the future.
And be blessed. As it settles.

we live up on a hill

As our lamp oil is wont for refill,
and darkness of souls linger,
sun rises on the bad and the good,
and rain falls on the just and the unjust.
And we adjust our mirrors, our blinds
and yet funny how we lose eyes
at horizon on our daily magic carpet rides.
Perhaps we can comprehend another hill,
or perhaps even the end of the world
as the sun rolls away.
If only right here we knew the beyond,
all the universe there is, we might realize
it is good to live as the saints here,
same as everywhere.

beyond time

saints are old
souls ever new

there are seeds
in the flower pot

each marigold
turns its face

by grace
in colors

not scrawled
in paints

saints
me and you

thought weeds
in breeds

but mercy
and peace

together
we reach

new

let us now see
how goes the infinite
simplifying

for as ever profound
goes every miracle
ever simple

as indescribable
the newborn
we now hold

simply
simply
all the world

and we now know
how blessed we are
to be

crossing beringia

Air is kind to the breast, snow broken as dust,
dew is salt to the feet, and everything feels like
luxury of hope, here where we now wander
this cold far-reaching strait, warm now enough

to pass under a sky wide as a white seabird
spreading its blanketing wings. Sun is hidden
under mask for us fragmented nomads
determinedly plodding onward.

On another plain, maybe I am so very different
than this. Or not. Here I am, as we all are,
with animal's wool around the neck,
and all the future ahead, simple, complex

as this meaning of every moment
and every moment next. Most of it only soon
taken for granted. But at this moment,
my young child takes my hand and asks nothing

but tightens the grip.

spun and woven

as clouds
are made

they sift
softly above

no matter
darkness

shepherd knows
true wool

upon verdant
valley

so goes
this gift of us

as gathered
together

no one alone
on the way

over cool green
we are made

world turns an ear

And, unseen Night Owl, you speak.

You speak.
Of the countless sleepless turns upon pillow I take,
of the prayers as merely childish visages of counted sheep.

Earth shall roll over, and morning shall come.

Till then, in the spin, missing the verdant, I count them again.
And the moon slides down the hill, the light of a dying font.
And the face feels the depth of suppleness in the grass
and I hear your voice of hopelessness mix with all the visages.

But from where you are, you may not be able to see
my fellow sheep faithfully climb back up the hill with me.
All of us soon fast asleep.
The Lord is our shepherd; there is nothing more we shall need.

they are like hills

Dreams are that way, it seems, never a bland matter of fact or overused, and they crest our sphere hard to hold just like rainbows blend to compliment nature's end. As if there is no end, but rather the beginning of a covenant. Ongoing. And always here.

They drift way up there, dreams, amidst palatial paintings of nearby heaven to here, and land in the gold of our hearts. And maybe as well land even in between ourselves, for dreams celebrate as they are, and where they are, and we hold on to each other.

little round top

In our civil war, here south of Gettysburg,
tell me, neighbor, are you cold as stone?
Or baked under the July sun?
Does your smell drift like mine as well?
Yes, like a mother's pie into pallor of the sky,
like all that is now unbreathable
as we wear our wool to war
and flex our chests, and count the gnats.
If only a cinnamon swirl,
this God forsaken, once lovely place,
rather than this kneaded lump of broken bone
and broken will.
Let us talk instead as if of the weather.
Say,
tell me of your time upon this particular hill?
Perhaps after words, I too can share mine.
Yes. After all, in time,
we are all again as once we were,
as children skipping stones.

declaration of interdependence

We hold these truths to be self-evident, that all are created equal, one by one by one, by all the world as one.

That we are endowed by our Creator to be unique and united. As such, when in the course of human events, let us help one another.

Neighbor, neighbor, mother, father, sister, brother, stranger. And the unending circle of the world has only just begun.

neighbor

And through the stained glass all of heaven is aglow,
for each of us to see exposed each other's eyes.
And our own.
We turn.

And the world this way unwinds its weight, rolling over
toward the window to feel the morning sun upon its hills.
So much stays still, stays the same, yet it all still moves.
We turn.

passerby

Tell me, Samaritan, in a world at war, as you walk this road,
what do you see from somewhere near, yet beyond to there
where horizon meets that borderline ahead? Commonplace
like sagebrush, and withered earth and face, here we are,
soon to meet. Beaten dry goes our voice in the desert. We

stand upon scorched sand and contemplate our present space,
and then warily only want to move ahead. We have soldiered
on to here where we are sentenced to be, with so many others
to see, so many of us yet still unseen, and so much hate, we
forget what we once looked like. But, up close, see, our slate

of stone has a face. And pain. Up close is where we are. Here,
up close, we look into each other's eyes no longer afar. See,
so much good we can do, maybe if only we knew. Maybe even
God is on this road, and if so, what would God do? Goodness,
do we ever dare to see God?! Here we are with a sudden view.

Of ourselves.

daily grind

I live in a whale.

Ribbed joists arch over me
as I sit and the vinyl sticks
to me amidst the bits
of broken fish
soon to go back to the sea
along with me.

I can make the most of this.

I can listen
to the heartbeat.
See the street dance
in the window.
And tap my feet.

And smile at the old lady
in the next seat.

little church on the big prairie

Heavy are skies. Sometimes, even in my confinement of trailer,
I can feel it. All that bouncing hail.

But church has joists across its ceiling holding up all that weight,
all that sagging bulk almost too much to carry. Time comes

and goes like summer clothes and broken umbrellos. Went and
saw God there today, maybe saw Her up close, close as a nose.

At the church. A stranger somehow applied some kind of grace
to my weathered face, maybe a nearby nun in nearby pew, yes,

with her simple but gentle sign of peace. A smile is a wide place.
Wide open land I would even later notice back at the trailer,

the cracked mirrors up the inside walls like storefronts waiting
for heaven and earth, as I opened the small door and saw myself.

supermarket aisle to aisle

We make our quick stop, hoping for the world.
Maybe at times seems we're far apart but shines
the grain at our soles as if we're only bowling
at neighboring alleys. And night cuts our face
the outside cold yet inside lights our hearts here
and goes warm in our more familiar shoes.

And I try to make my valid points like any
bowling pins standing, waiting and hoping maybe
you think of us as no gutter ball, but the world,
maybe miraculously meant to be, a perfect frame,
maybe, or despite others disbelief, a 7-10 split
of cans of creamed beef to an unbelievable spare.

And, yes, overflows our baskets, the phenomenon.

More than just a few fish, but a big ol' honeydew.
All the world to share. With a dime to spare.
We are. So blessed. To be.

fields of the rich

Hide the world like a squirrel. Don't hide the squirrel.
Find it again when no one might notice, not even you.
And not even the unhidden squirrel now next to you.
So much is hidden, inevitably becoming only the world.

It is a tall silo, filled to the top, so to see all the green.
If we could hasten to the hill country and sit up there,
as the golden knolls crease, and the treasures unfold,
up high it is so easy to see all that we possess. And yet,

we might easily overlook what is in front of us instead.
Funny, funny how things can become numb. Or not.
One would think the truly rich shall truly know
what is funny. At this, the squirrel only darts away.

Published by Grand Little Things, 2020

soils and spoils

Earth turns it face to go to sleep. To rest in peace.
And so many poor souls feel detached from the pillow.
Every day people fall off the world.
If only they knew an outstretched hand to save them.
The proximity from all the extraterrestrial display
to here upon our terrestrial place, this our shared face,
is distance we could walk on water simply with faith,
not just a surface frozen over, not just cold outer space,
but the everyday void we seemingly put into place
where bounty is numbed, and the roots are pulled,
and we forget mercy remains only a moment away.

earth breathes

From its belly, it lifts and falls, hardens and softens,
closes and opens. See the canyon and find my heart
somewhere at its floor.
Not to stay. That is not what a heart is for.

Rather, to give birth.
See me soon sing at the magnolia branch, silk as air.
See me soon open armed at the mountain top, not to stop,
but from there to soar. Same with you and yours.

See me
and see you
in the highlands of clouds, bending upright in a bouquet,
awe of ours.

unearthed

was once sadness possibly, callous possibly,
or joy, life goes on, worn back to earth, sifting
to sky, things mingle like that with past and then

God bends time as if time can go and unwind and
some things are made to that way last mercifully but
sometimes our minds go unwise to just up and hide

in our wide ignorance, overlooking this dreamland
not necessarily with malice, but awry in deep want
for our very own filled chalice this moment this now

ever alight despite ephemeral ice while we question
what endures within even this just found and grimed,
aged and seemingly otherwise useless slippery grail.

point of view

We all have our own ball. We share it though.
Globe presents itself to view its space, its surge
of messages to all our eyes in passages diverse.

Each at a separate pace, we each unroll our face.

thinker

How much is given?
How much is taken?
How much is allowed to be?
I think, and therefore
I am like a ram.
What of the lion, and the lame,
the lamb, and the caged?

Count the ways of various prodigy.
Am I more than the matter of a brain?
Count the ways of ingenuity.
So much is human majesty.
What is not meant to be taken away?
Open the mind beyond the world
and count the ways.

Say a soul is greater than all of these.
What lingers at the surface,
and ever deep?
What then might we always find?
I am a woman,
and I am a man.
I am in the image of the Divine.

portrait of Salvator Mundi

And there is a smile of the Great Spirit
wide as Lake Winnipesaukee.
It's there in the window frame peek-a-boo
where all the sky goes thru.

Again, there on that building's sides
as rush hour crowd boomerangs.
There, in glass of the blurring bus,
and up on that pole noted as lost.

And inside that tidy Cape Cod
reflecting upon a family's supper table.
And there, that stride of color at the strip
upon the bowling alley floor.

There on the slab of concrete
where sleeps silently that homeless lady.
And here in mirror canvas of this morning
as I unveil a face for today.

self-portrait

a window
open
to see
God's love and
endless creativity
all of humanity

beyond vast

while in all the marvel we physically are
there is far more beyond the mortal
beyond all time and beyond gender
beyond what is flesh and beyond all limits

goes the soul

for love is boundless as made and duplicated
and thus each of us goes precious infinitum
eternally blessed and ever internally near

if only we knew

before mindlessly throwing it all far away

empty space

and
as filaments unwind away
as our orbits get cut down
to less than their threads
if not for dignity
if not for that love
what was
what is
what can be
comes down to this

if any singular one of us
sifts
unloved

siphoned

away

then

we all are still

empty

closed-mindedness

Yes, the world is a big place. And yet, sometimes we are too big for it. Beware our fanciful mess of walls that may appear as if horizon of statement, as if High Sierra itself, and its tall accounts. Sky flares to smooth over the tar upon all the world's roofs, and smooth over those roofless too, those with not even rusted tin above heads lacking any supposed wealth of knowledge while the supposed learned may now show how to properly open not only a mind, but a heart. Or not. Truth is, the smartest of smart know what to do with knowledge, and the rest of us, well, we all may not know so very much. Except, hopefully, that all good things are possible. That may be a proper start.

shipbuilders and the world

Ship in a bottle on a table, and we are now able to see the sea.
Ship in a bottle on a table, and all the world is within reach.
Here, where windows sway sun, yes, the bend of land is near.

It is a supper table, and a blessed family circles, nourishing.
See a wide world here at hand. The daisy too seems to sway.
Sea cannot be squeezed into a bottle, but to a degree can.

Look closer. It is not a real ship upon a real and raging sea.
Yet, upon the gaze, one may still feel the wide ocean's roar.
See, land ho! Primed for discovery. And here we now are.

Ship in a bottle on a table, and let us disembark, to be here.
What can we now make of the world faraway and near.
What shall it make of us?

more than all tides rage

Talk with me with eyes across our table.
More than our tide, our tide, our tide, we are.
Put aside the changing tide, all that drifts.
Feel the warm glow as peace upon the face.

Sun now stands still to allow earth to see,
to run, disavow all dearth, fall asleep.
One by one we cow with roped girth faintly.
What has begun, now we just unearth deep.

Seas can kangaroo course, yet we quit quick.
Land sees centrifugal force as we fade.
In gold, bees imbue, endure tours drastic.
We somehow seize few reins to tame horse staid.

Still, sun stands clear, hiding its face at night.
Stars thrill with moon near as rides heaven's eye.
Flyers shill no fear as wings bide time's flight.
Ours is free will, dear more than all tides rage.

Undone breeze, fill us strong; birth source, guide song.
Swung monkeys till gust flung forth, we are sprung.
So, put aside all the sea tangled words.
Talk with me with eyes across our table.

same boat

And now we are here,
this world we share,
upon an ark that sits
in this desert
waiting for rain again.

How blessed together are we
for the dove at the window.
But are we ready
to embark for peace
if it doesn't rain again?

We may just need to change,
to disembark,
and see each other with mercy,
this sea, this sea,
of ourselves.

travel partners

Somewhere we may say this is your land, and this is my land,
this patch by patch screened beyond the open endless sea
through our rose colored blinds, just a pyrotechnic display
maybe in our minds. Buds on branches will bloom in due time.
I hear harvest is noble and true, unless Ice Age returns soon.

The raven and dove give of self looking for the telltale sign.
Pimentos are holed to souls in green olives, and rather exposed.
The plains I have learned are open wide. Nowhere to hide.
As for us, accepting of another, and the self, we can make it.
Two by two to walk the plank and not drown, but to get around.

So, let us be seasick, but ready. Tell me about yourself.
We sure are similar. You're almost a mirror of me, one or two
doubloons. Genuine, not fake. Say this for heaven's sake—
even though Noah's name tags sometimes can hide the heart,
let us be what can be said about souls exposed from olives.

Let us both show the red pepper within, and yet still get along.

in a good place

There is space where you are.

And gravity.

Gravity is a necessary prerequisite
for a body of water.

You are mostly water, but
a heart can be empty.

Allow the raindrops from above
and see what soon runs in rivers.

same place

There is a boilerplate at our feet, bold and smooth as our names,
now suddenly varied as the wrinkled landscape of an afraid face.
This land of marble tombstone is one we may never truly escape.

See, we saw the day disappear into distance, a rock into water,
a rocket into outer space, or just a dinosaur. We let ourselves go.
We let stars, ours, drift across our eyes until our windows cried.

Hand in hand, we visit now to see all that has happened since.
There upon the ground, now hardened, our distinct footprints.
And we still laugh, for we are indeed still home after all of this.

license plates

In the lot of license plates, I am one.
My particular symbols differentiate me
here when parking, or in a jam,
or on the run.
You've got yours.
I've got mine.

We may share shades,
hail from same state,
clack like cymbals parking space to space,
and not be all that different face to face.
Generally, we're all same shape.
But, each, a unique one.

all the world

By the carousel,
we may wonder of the worker there
and if wonder of the world remains.

Wonder is such a trite word.
Wonder if so goes all the world.
Mood swings may be understandable.

Is she overworked and thus numbed?
Does she remember her own first ride?
Does she still take time to swirl?

There is a chain of command,
and we are all links, needing each.
In front of her is all the world.

Same as ours.
We are all sharing this ride.
A gift we experience together.

I see her licensed badge—
Susan Bogert Warner.
Didn't she write *Wide, Wide World*?!

I trust her outstretched hand
and present her my ticket.
And allow myself the wonder.

view from 44th floor

Little machines are silent as the sun opens
as if it too may very well speak but doesn't.
City sprouts its mirrors and sun again sends
train yokes snaking burdens above the bugs.
The strung aqueducts lift the trains far away.
And graffiti upon them says little or so much,
mostly misunderstood as gibberish scribble
running and unread as such, as the bugs rush
gathered and separated, then gathered again
as only all of us.

bigness

Muscled arms hold up our weight,
and world sinks through holes.
Bullets have pierced the Roman columns
of our forgotten city.
Our reddened clay hands run
like ruins, and despite time that runs,
and despite rivers that divide and
take their crime carrying Styx
and stones of ourselves, we go
again to war remembering too little,
widening our way but not realizing
we may be indeed running late,
while simply wandering. The world
is a big road to unravel. Maybe
it would be big of ourselves to stop
and ask each other for directions.

big as billboards

Marketers unravel our roads of life like a read, like a magazine.
The writers want it to be simple for their purposes of purchase,
even if to some of us sometimes sadly incomprehensible.

Vision relies on the size of our inner eyes, even if blind,
with sensibility enough to read beyond the lines,
through the lines, atop the lines, and even underneath.

Sometimes, the world is all subliminal and we dwindle too small.
Sometimes, star struck and all too numb, we forget how to read.
Sometimes, we lose the way through the woods, for the signs.

Sometimes, we drift too worldly.
Sometimes, the world is so unnoticeable.
Sometimes, we pull up the rags tight to our chins as we sleep.

Sometimes, the signs are too easy to see, and we disappear.
Sometimes, we just stay unseen.
That simple.

All along, we are the world, just passing by, on its way.
Leaving it behind, for we belong to a wider place.
Hopefully following those road signs, big as loving eyes.

map

You are here, so it says, in latitude and longitude.
And so I wish to be as well.
And all of Vancouver pulls together the sky.
Unfolds the textured face as if by wipe of Veronica.

We go, the poor and yet endure the bountiful as rich,
for we are not left weak upon this place, but fortified
beyond our station and within as well, refreshed
in Whom we live and move and have our being.

Yes, we shall fall, and shall arise, we of paradise.
Stubborn the white hair and yet again surrendering.
And the sun now shall lift just like us and shall set.
Love is no earthen way of wither to let us forget.

Earth is far more than just the Pacific Northwest.
You are everywhere, but, yes, specifically here,
in the texture 49.2827° N, 123.1207° W,
as all of Vancouver faces the sky to smile wide.

manhattan rain

And listen, if you will,
upon the mirrored gleam,
as life emanates rain's refrain.
Listen for your name,
distinct as a drop

and yet a rainfall just the same.

turtle

She lost her way in the water,
or maybe found it
now as an island.

Her spirit is more than shell,
and always was.
This, she did not know but now does.

And see how Time moves.
And Time is a mountain.
And Time is a feather.

Sometimes, a long climb.
Sometimes, flight.
Sometimes, unbearable weight

shared as a compassionate place
while angels we have heard
inside count the stars pass by.

time in her field

She tends a sprawling farm that spreads to horizon.
Grows peas. Time flies. And she has a shed full of clocks.
Maybe hundreds up and down the walls.
Some face up, some down. Some with amputated hand and arm.
Some, done. Not sure how many work, maybe one or two,
or none. Funny how we stare at a broken clock, at its silence.

If only we could just open our ears across the air to also listen.
She says sky has a heartbeat.
Some think she's a cuckoo, but she's ever so clever. Yes,
she tends a sprawling farm that spreads to horizon.
And, every day she is never up late with so much to do.
She knows her rooster at top of shed has first sight of sun.

lasts

She says some things always end. Period.
There is a flashpoint, and souls catch fire.
While here after a while away, just caskets.
There is a dousing within each and all of us.
There is time that slips away, and what stays?
As if a miracle of five loaves and two fish,
and mercy for seconds, we remain in baskets.
There is an ongoing song, she forever says.
As if in the blues, the rhythm still can remain.

We can let ourselves go vulnerable in skin
and write tomes as if on parchment, classics.
Another thousand years go by and we remain.
She says we can wait for what has no stop.
She says we can rush for what has no stop.
Lasts, all along, our need for Love, she says.
By God, lasts all along, our need for Love.
It feels so good to begin, even in the ashes.
She beams and says new things always begin.

Because Love has no end.

take away the stone

I am no Sisyphus, and yet the daily heaviness
overwhelms me.
I am no Poe, and yet the chamber door is before me.
I am no blind man, and yet my eye is good as closed.

I exist behind seemingly an impenetrable divide.
My impediment is not of braided bread,
not of things I may never comprehend, yet instead
a mountain to move.

And how can anyone bear the expected stench?
Am I good as dead as any Lazarus? If so, let it be.
How indeed might such a mountain move?
Jesus has spoken, and what has Jesus said?

love one another

And believe, After all, we all
stretch to seize and take lost dreams, mine and yours,
close as others, and we each suffer occasional closed eyes,
deceived in this dark place, a place of an enigmatic past,
grain upon solitary grain, a place of amassed sand, waterless,
and too few a desert shoot. Unless there is more to Truth.

We have run from God, and yet,
God is ever somewhere near with mercy.

Somehow, mountains are made to move, and faith matters.
Sea shells twirl into shape, and God plays amidst the manatees.
Across the land, despite all the current survival of the fittest,
the lion and the lamb, made to sit together, shall one day again.

Somehow in all of this, here is humanity, in the image of Love,
this way made.

Love is in our DNA.

And somewhere in the lineage we beget and intertwine
a connectedness in the way we give in to find ourselves
an amazement, and so goes our ancient ongoing longing
for the belonging to what is without end spined in this Truth.

despite space debris

Coming home should be magical,
even for just a flicker of hope,
and remain. Someone left a heart
on the sofa. We shall cradle it. So
much tends to dissipate, but now,
unafraid, let this be a happy place
where love shows its happy face.

This heart has a familiar face. Let us
savor memory of the site, the sure
landing pad, and target it, not with
a nuclear device, but maybe a wide
welcoming familiar face of our own.
After all, who shall arrive to pick up
their heart, if not to meet face to face?

It all comes down to it, the sharing
of space. All of sky rides outer space
an overflowing abundant rhyme now
in its disarray, the never redundant
shooting stars travelling the line here
to a place where amidst all the mess,
there is always space to sit.

sveiki

see

warming each face
a smile
blessed to be
wherever it is we are
together

yes see

how the world can be

a beautiful place

quarry

And in the end,
it has come down to this—

I've searched for peace
under every heavy stone

and have finally realized my weight,
for there it is under my own.

unwind

and when this darkness seems to have no end
when purpose seems to be dead like doldrums

when present silence seems to deafen all friends
and the wind from truth's voice goes silent

and all who labor are lost in unrest
and all who are lost are labored in distress

and all solemnity has slipped through the hand
beyond any semblance even for a heroic reinvent

and as scripture says, darkness covers the earth

yes

even then

as we unroll the shroud and reveal our faith
blessed are we as turns the stone

www.ingramcontent.com/pod-product-compliance
Lightning Source LLC
Chambersburg PA
CBHW022201160726
48282CB00024B/275
* 9 7 8 8 1 8 2 5 3 7 6 5 1 *